Maps and mapping

with Suki West, cartographer

Jinny Johnson

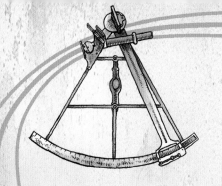

KINGFISHER

Kingfisher Publications Plc
New Penderel House
283–288 High Holborn
London WC1V 7HZ
www.kingfisherpub.com

First published by Kingfisher Publications Plc 2007
1 3 5 7 9 10 8 6 4 2

1TR/0307/SNPTHAI/SCHOY(SCHOY)/157MA/C

A CIP catalogue record for this book is available from the British Library.

ISBN 978 07534 1417 0

Managing editor: Carron Brown
Senior designers: Peter Clayman, Carol Ann Davis
Picture research manager: Cee Weston-Baker
DTP co-ordinator: Catherine Hibbert
Senior production controller: Lindsey Scott
Proofreader and indexer: Polly Goodman

Printed in Thailand

Contents

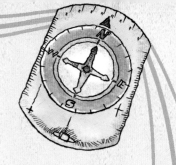
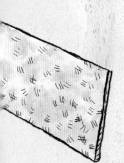

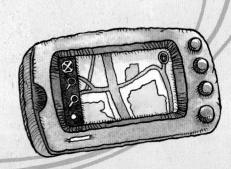

Meet your guide

Hello, my name is Suki West. I love looking at all sorts of maps, from a plan of a town to a globe of the world. I am a cartographer, which means it's my job to make maps. A map is a way of showing an area – anything from the universe to a park, or the street where you live. You can even make a map of your own house or room.

"I can't imagine a life without maps. HOW would we find our way around the world?"

The earliest world map that still exists was made more than 2,500 years ago in Babylon. It was drawn on a clay tablet and shows Babylon at the centre of the world.

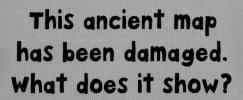

This ancient map has been damaged. What does it show?

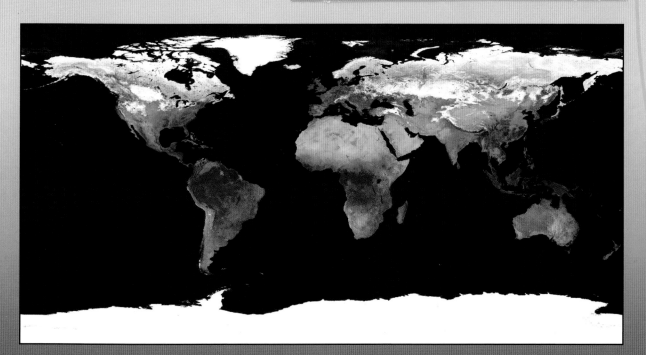

world map from 2006, made using satellite images

Why we need maps

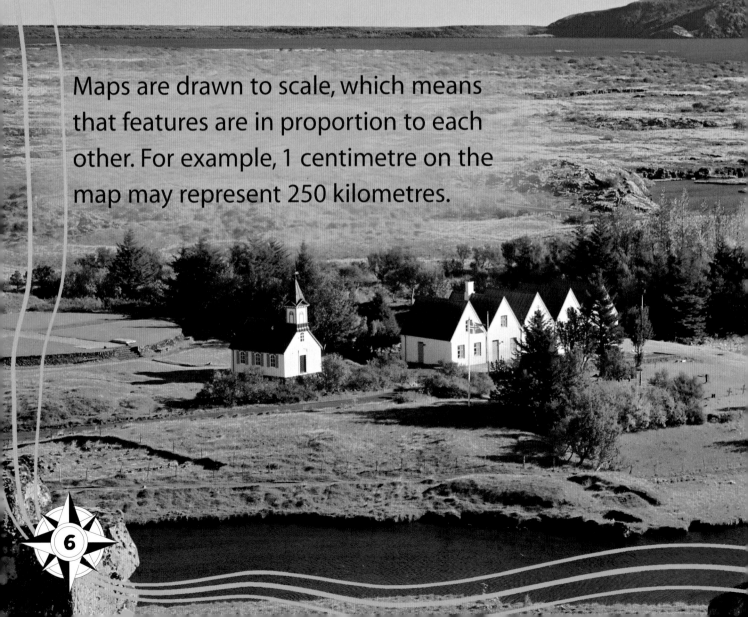

A map shows part of the world on a flat surface, usually a piece of paper. A map of a country shows its shape, the countries around it, and features such as the main towns. A map of a small part of a country can show more detail, such as hills, woodland and roads.

Maps are drawn to scale, which means that features are in proportion to each other. For example, 1 centimetre on the map may represent 250 kilometres.

"When I walk in the country, I take a detailed, large-scale map where one centimetre may represent only 250 metres."

Look at my map. Does it show where I should cross the river?

The first maps

When I travel, I look at maps of the places I'm going to visit, but how did people manage long ago? The Romans are famous for building an amazing network of roads, but did you know they also made maps? By the 4th century CE, Roman maps showed roads, as well as distances and information such as places to stay. These must have been the first travel guides!

Roman milestone in Switzerland

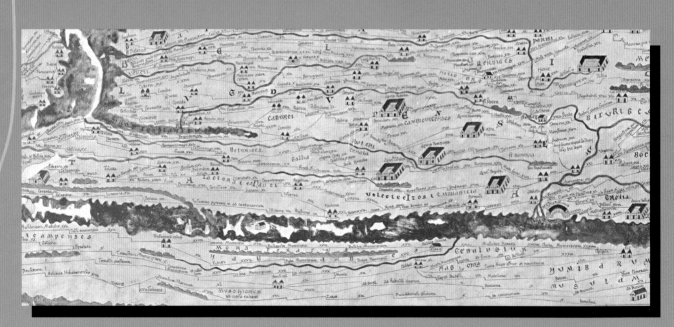

Roman map from the 4th century CE, showing buildings

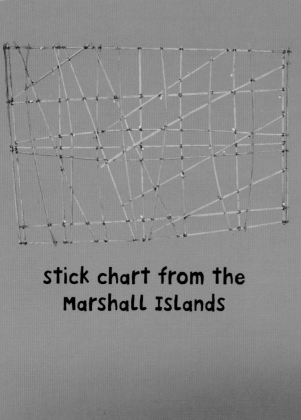

stick chart from the
Marshall Islands

Hundreds of years ago in the Pacific Ocean, islanders made stick charts from palm fibres. These showed ocean currents and wave patterns. The positions of islands were marked by shells.

"It's quite difficult to follow these early maps. Each shell and palm fibre has a meaning."

Maps and explorers

Today, there is a lot of information to help us make maps, including pictures of the earth from space. We know exactly what the world looks like. But years ago map-making was very different. When explorers went on voyages of discovery, they had only a rough idea of the shape of the land. As they travelled, they studied coastlines and other features, and added more detail to maps.

"Like the early explorers, I use a compass to find out where north is."

world map from 1570

compass

Explorers used sextants and compasses to help them navigate across oceans. For example, by using a sextant to measure the angle of the sun in the sky, they could work out where they were on an ocean chart.

sextant

Ship sailed by the English explorer Sir Francis Drake (c. 1540-1596)

Mapping the world

The world is round, so a map on a globe is more true to life than a flat map. To help us find places, map-makers divide the world with imaginary lines, called lines of latitude and longitude. The Equator is a line of latitude that circles the earth half-way between the North and South poles. East and west are divided by lines of longitude. They run north to south and meet at the poles.

South American parrot

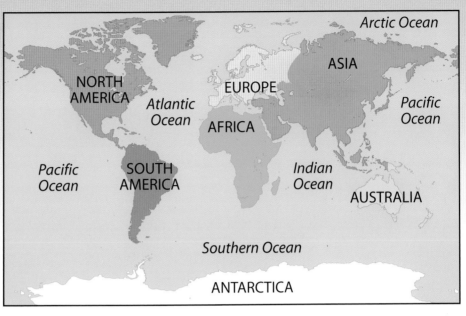

			Arctic Ocean

Map labels: NORTH AMERICA, *Atlantic Ocean*, EUROPE, ASIA, AFRICA, *Pacific Ocean*, *Pacific Ocean*, SOUTH AMERICA, *Indian Ocean*, AUSTRALIA, *Southern Ocean*, ANTARCTICA

Only a quarter of the earth's surface is land. The rest is covered with oceans, seas, lakes and rivers. The world's main areas of land are the seven continents.

"You will always find ice and snow at the poles!"

Which way to the North Pole and the polar bears?

13

making the world flat

When we make a map of the world, some countries appear bigger than they really are, but others look smaller. This is because we are flattening out shapes that are on a rounded surface. The different ways of making flat maps of the world are called projections. Two of the most popular are the Mercator projection and the Peters projection.

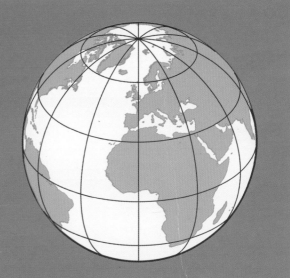

How can a rounded globe be made into a flat map?

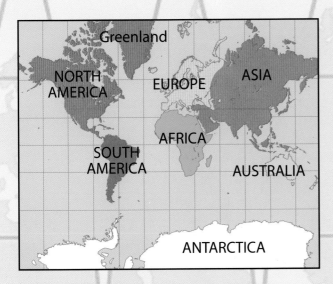

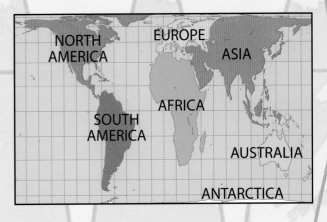

On a Mercator projection, areas such as Europe, Antarctica and Greenland appear much larger than they are.

The Peters projection shows the continents in the right proportion to each other, but distorts their shape, making them look longer and thinner than they really are.

"one important use of flat maps is in atlases. An atlas is a book of maps of different parts of the world."

Mapping countries

Cartographers like me make a lot of different sorts of maps. One very important kind shows where cities, towns and borders are. This is called a political map. A map of a large area, such as the continent of Africa, might show where all the different countries are.

political map of Africa

Maps showing mountains and other types of land are called physical, or relief, maps. High areas, such as mountains, are a darker colour than low areas.

Hokkaido

● Sapporo

0   100   200   300   400   500 kilometres

0   100   200   300 miles

H o n s h u

Mount Fuji ▲   ■TOKYO

Kobe   ● Nagoya
   ●
   Osaka

Shikoku

Kyushu

physical map of Japan

"The highest mountain in Japan is Mount Fuji. It is 3,776 metres tall. Can you find it on the map?"

Mapping mountains

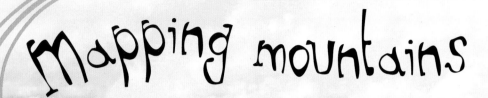

When I go hillwalking, I take a map that shows me exactly what to expect. This is called a topographic map. To make one you need to know the heights of all the hills and mountains in the area, and how steep they are.

"If contour lines are drawn close together, that means the mountain is steep and there's a hard climb ahead."

On this kind of map, mountains are shown
with special lines, called contour lines.
These are drawn to link all the areas
that are the same height.

19

Your home town

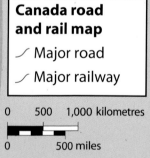

Another part of my job is to make maps showing roads in a country and special maps showing streets in a town.

A road map has to show every road, and mark which ones are motorways, major roads or smaller roads, so that people can find their way without getting lost. A road map usually shows railways too.

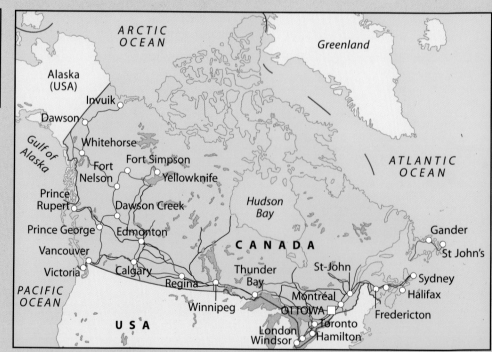

Canada road and rail map

⟋ Major road

⟋ Major railway

0   500   1,000 kilometres

0   500 miles

ARCTIC OCEAN

Greenland

Alaska (USA)

Invuik

Dawson

Whitehorse

Gulf of Alaska

Fort Simpson

Fort Nelson

Yellowknife

Prince Rupert

Dawson Creek

Hudson Bay

ATLANTIC OCEAN

Prince George

Edmonton

CANADA

Gander

St John's

Vancouver

Victoria

Calgary

Thunder Bay

St-John

Sydney

Regina

Halifax

PACIFIC OCEAN

Winnipeg

Montréal

OTTOWA

Fredericton

USA

London Windsor

Toronto Hamilton

Toronto city

Toronto city map key

P Car park
Train station
Airport
Police station
+ Hospital
Church
Synagogue
Park
Housing area
Business area

Map labels

University of
Toronto

Bathurst Street

Toronto
General Hospital

College Street

Toronto
Western Hospital

Dundas Street West

International
Toronto Centre

Union
Station

Queen Street West

King Street West

Roger's Centre

Belwoods Park

Direct Energy
Centre

Corporation
Park

Toronto Inner
Harbour

Lake Shore Boulevard West

West
Island

East
Island

Toronto City
Centre Airport

Lake Ontario

0   500   1,000 metres

0   3,000 feet

"Do you want the train station? Look at this key to see which symbol to find on the map."

Street maps need to show all street names, even tiny ones. Important places, such as stations and churches, are marked too, using little symbols. A box, called a key, is put at the side of the map. It explains what all the different colours and symbols mean.

Information maps

Special kinds of maps are used to display information and make it easy to understand. Cartographers may colour a map to show where the highest rainfall is in a country or where crops are grown. This map of Australia shows where the most people live. The darker the colour, the more people there are living in that area.

Very few people live in the centre of Australia.

Australia population key
people per 2.5 square kilometres

☐	0 to 1
☐	average of 1
☐	1 to 9
☐	10 to 99
☐	100 to 999
☐	1,000 to 10,000

0   200   400   600   800   1,000 kilometres

0   100   300   500   700 miles

Most Australians live in big cities on the coast.

22

"When I go to a theme park I always make sure I get the map or plan, so I can find my favourite rides!"

Weather forecasters need maps too. You'll see a map of your country whenever you watch the weather report on television. The forecaster will point out on the map where rain is going to fall and how warm or cool your area is going to be.

Mapping space

Early maps of the Moon were made by using telescopes and drawing what could be seen. The names of many craters on the Moon date from the 17th century when people first did this. Today, more detailed maps are created using spacecraft that orbit the Moon and take pictures of its surface. Robotic vehicles have also landed on the Moon and some planets.

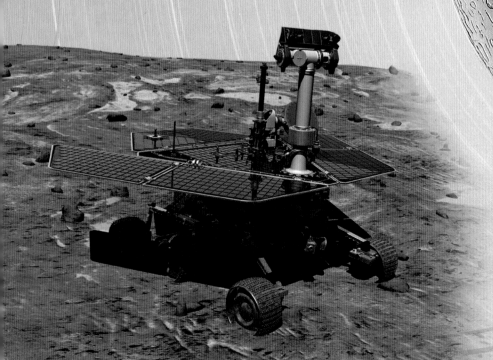

Mars Rover
mapping Mars

Saturn

Saturn's moon, Titan

Cassini-Huygens spacecraft

Even planets millions of kilometres away, such as Jupiter and Saturn, are now being mapped. The Cassini-Huygens spacecraft is finding out more about Saturn and its rings and moons.

"I love to look at the Moon. I wish I could travel there to make my own map of its surface."

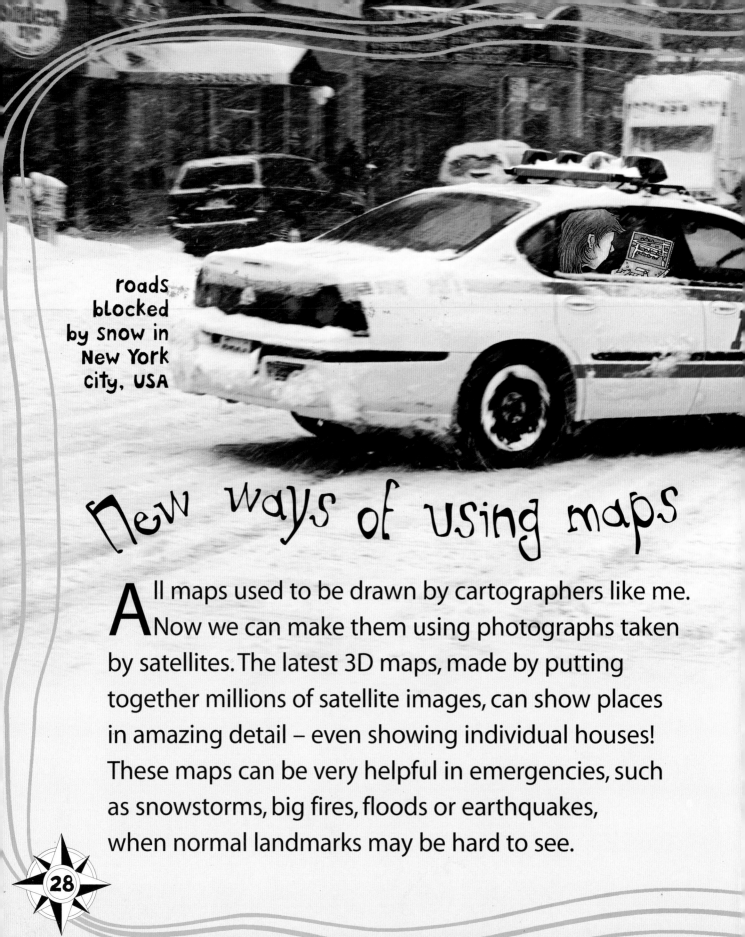

roads
blocked
by snow in
New York
city, USA

New ways of using maps

All maps used to be drawn by cartographers like me. Now we can make them using photographs taken by satellites. The latest 3D maps, made by putting together millions of satellite images, can show places in amazing detail – even showing individual houses! These maps can be very helpful in emergencies, such as snowstorms, big fires, floods or earthquakes, when normal landmarks may be hard to see.

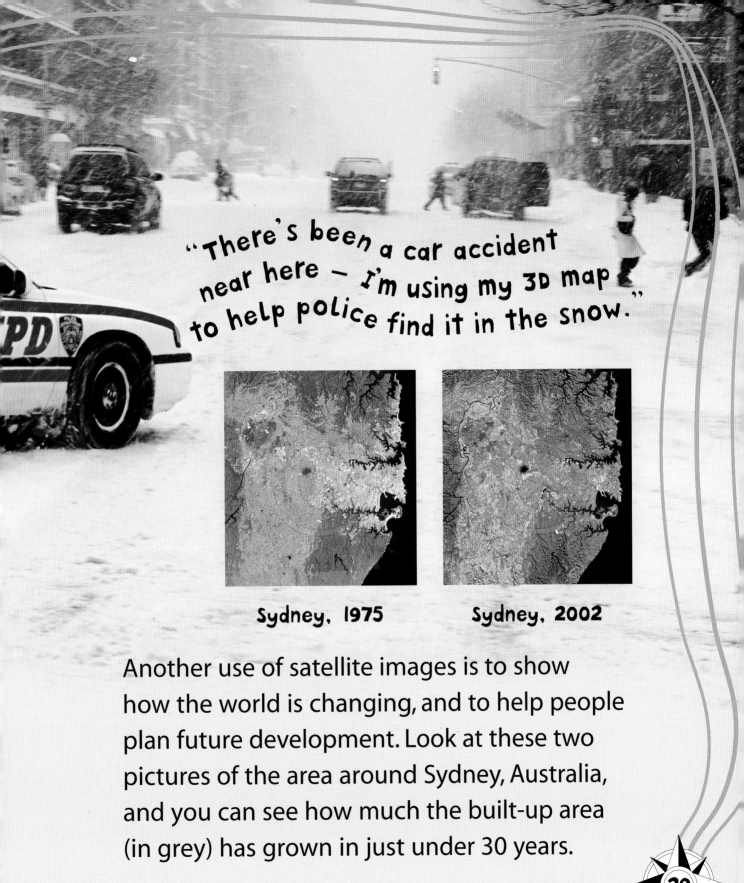

"There's been a car accident near here — I'm using my 3D map to help police find it in the snow."

Sydney, 1975   Sydney, 2002

Another use of satellite images is to show how the world is changing, and to help people plan future development. Look at these two pictures of the area around Sydney, Australia, and you can see how much the built-up area (in grey) has grown in just under 30 years.

Glossary

atlas A book of maps.

cartography The science of making maps. A person who makes maps is called a cartographer.

chart A kind of map used by ship and aeroplane pilots to help them find their way.

compass An instrument that shows direction. The magnetized needle on a compass always points north.

continent One of the earth's main areas of land. There are seven continents – Asia, Africa, North America, South America, Antarctica, Europe and Australia.

Equator An imaginary line around the middle of the earth, halfway between the North and South poles.

globe A map of the world, shaped like a ball.

large scale Big enough to show a lot of detail. The larger the scale of a map, the more detail it can show. On a good walking map, for example, 250 metres in real life is 1 centimetre on the map.

lines of latitude Imaginary circles drawn around the earth at regular distances between the Equator and the poles. The lines are parallel to the Equator.

lines of longitude Imaginary lines drawn from the north to south of the earth. The lines meet at the poles and are farthest apart at the Equator.

poles The far north and south of the earth.

political map A map that shows countries and their boundaries, as well as main towns and cities.

projection The way a cartographer shows the round earth on a flat map. There are different projections, but they all change the shape of some countries.

proportion The relationship between the sizes of things. If one thing on a map is shown at 1 per cent of its actual size, everything else on the map must be shown at the same proportion.

relief map A map that is shaded to show how high or low the land is.

satellite A machine that is sent into space to orbit (go round) the earth or another planet and send information and pictures back to earth.

scale Every map has a scale that shows how big something on the map is compared to how it is in real life.

sonar (**so**und **n**avigation **a**nd **r**anging) A way of using sound echoes to help navigate under water.

Index

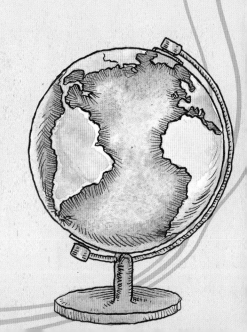

Acknowledgements

The publisher would like to thank the following for permission to reproduce their material. Every care has been taken to trace copyright holders. However, if there have been unintentional omissions or failure to trace copyright holders, we apologize and will, if informed, endeavour to make corrections in any future edition.

Key: *b* = bottom, *c* = centre, *l* = left, *r* = right, *t* = top

4 Judith Collins/Alamy; 5*t* British Museum/Bridgeman Art Library; 5*b* Earth Observatory/NASA; 6–7 Peter Adams/zefa/Corbis; 8*tr* Sandro Vannini/Corbis; 8*b* Musee de la Poste/Bridgeman Art Library; 9*tl* British Museum/Heritage Image Partnership; 9*b* Douglas Peebles/Corbis; 10–11 Joel W. Rogers/ Corbis; 10*b* Dagli Orti/The Art Archive; 11*tr* Taxi/Getty Images; 11*tc* Hemeira Technologies/Alamy; 12*l* Photonica/Getty Images; 12–13 Riser/Getty Images; 18–19 Photographer's Choice/Getty Images; 21*tr* Rudy Sulgan/Corbis; 22*tr* Larry Williams/zefa/Corbis; 22*b* Jose Fuste Raga/Corbis; 22–23 Corbis; 24–25 National Oceanic & Atmospheric Administration/US Dept of Commerce; 25*t* W Haxby/ Lamont-Doherhty Earth Observatory/Science Photo Library; 26–27 Louie Psihoyos/Corbis; 26 NASA; 27 European Space Agency/NASA; 28–29 Alan Schein/Alamy; 28*c* Earth Observatory/NASA.

The publisher would like to thank the following illustrators:
Peter Bull 26–27; Sebastian Quigley 18–19, 24–25; Lyn Stone (Suki West and incidentals throughout); Peter Winfield 5*t*, 7*bl*, 12–13, 13*t*, 14*b*, 15*t*, 16, 17, 20, 21*tl*, 22*c*, 23*tl*.